Pontifical Administration
of the Patriarchal Basilica of Saint Paul

The Basilica of
Saint Paul
Outside the Walls

Libreria Editrice Vaticana

Texts and Captions
Anna Maria Cerioni
Roberto Del Signore

Translation
John A. Abruzzese

Photographs
www.studiorifrazioni.it

Layout and Printing
Grafiche Grilli srl - Foggia

Cover Illustrations
Antoniazzo Romano, Fresco of Saint Paul
and View of the Façade of the Basilica and Portico

Back Cover Illustration
Detail of Apse Mosaic

ISBN 88-209-4619X

Presentation

In 1988, the Pontifical Administration of the Patriarchal Basilica of Saint Paul sponsored the publication of a lengthy treatise on the Basilica dedicated to the Apostle of the Gentiles, under the auspices of Carlo Pietrangeli, General Director of Monuments, Museums and Pontifical Galleries, who was assisted by renowned scholars. Subsequently, in 1991, Anna Maria Cerioni and Roberto Del Signore were asked to compose an historical-artistic guidebook which appeared in five languages.

This second edition, available in the same five languages and utilizing the text of the initial edition, adds a new series of splendid photographs which permits a glimpse of the beauty of this imposing Basilica, reconstructed after the fire of 1823. The pilgrim is struck by the Basilica's size, the preciousness of its building materials and the various artifacts remaining from the old Basilica and adjoining Benedictine Abbey, among which are the mosaics, the Byzantine door, the Altar Canopy of Arnolfo, the Easter Candlestick and the superb Cosmati cloister.

The present publication, with its completely new photographic layout, has a twofold purpose: to increase devotion to the Apostle of the Gentiles and to make the beauty of the Basilica better known.

Many pilgrims visit the Basilica to pray at the tomb of the Apostle, located under the high altar. All experience the mysterious fascination of the unique figure of St. Paul, Imitator of Christ par excellence. As a courageous, untiring missionary, he carried the Gospel to the entire world of his time, pursuing a course of well over 7,800 kilometers on foot and 9,000 by ship. St. Paul himself states: "I have become all things to all men, that I might by all means save some" (1 Cor 9:23). Nothing could extinguish his apostolic zeal. For him, even difficulties were a source of joy, as he tells the Corinthians: "For the sake of Christ, I am content with weaknesses, insults, hardships, persecutions and calamities" (2 Cor 12:10).

For those who encounter him in the Basilica built in his honor, and also for those who in whatever way are engaged in his venture in life and spirit, all that remains is to accept St. Paul's invitation: "Be imitators of me, as I am of Christ" (1 Cor 11:1).

Rome, 25 January 2003
The Conversion of St. Paul

+ Francesco Gioia, *Archbishop*
Pontifical Administrator
of the Patriarcal Basilica of Saint Paul

1. An Historical Overview

The Basilica of Saint Paul Outside the Walls, the second largest Roman church after the Vatican, stands on the *Via Ostiense*, about 2 kilometres from the Aurelian Walls, near the left bank of the Tiber.

Standing on the burial place of Saint Paul, the Apostle of the Gentiles, the site has never ceased to be the destination of pilgrims and ordinary visitors. From the very first Holy Year in 1300, it has been included in the jubilee itinerary for indulgences and is one of the basilicas where the opening of the Holy Door is celebrated.

The present edifice was built over a period spanning more than a century, following the disastrous fire of July, 1823 which half-destroyed the grandiose ancient Basilica. Until that time, the building had remained substantially intact.

The *Liber Pontificalis* attributes to the munificence of Constantine the construction of a place of worship on the site of the *cella memoriae* of Saint Paul, marked from the 5th century by the two famous marble slabs bearing the inscription *"Paulo Apostolo Martyri"*. Saint Paul was buried in the small graveyard adjacent to *Via Ostiense*, not far from the area called *Ad Aquas Salvias* (known today as "Three Fountains"), the site of his martyrdom in 67 AD.

The apse of the Constantine's Church was probably situated opposite the present one, standing on a road which is generally recognised to be the ancient route of the *Via Ostiense*. The original Church must have been very modest in size, since the Emperors Valentinian II, Theodosius and Arcadius decided to design a new place of worship. Building started some time between 384 and 386 and was completed under Honorius, as the mosaic inscription on the triumphal arch indicates: "THEODOSIUS COEPIT PERFECIT HONORIUS AULAM / DOCTORIS MUNDI SACRATAM CORPORE PAULI."

The Basilica "of the Three Emperors", with its immense quadrangular portico with a fountain in the centre, had five entrances (at present, there are seven) and was quite similar to the 19th century reconstruction.

The first restoration took place in the middle of the 5th century under

Saint Paul, fresco of the workshop of Antoniazzo Romano (15th Century), from the lunette in the passageway between the Gregorian Room (Basilica entrance, Via Ostiense) and the Baptistry.

Leo I (440-461), perhaps as a result of a natural disaster. This Pope also began to decorate with mosaics the recently fortified triumphal arch of the Basilica. The series of paintings on the walls of the nave, depicting scenes from the Old and New Testament (Cavallini was to repaint them at the end of the 13th century), and the beginning of the first series of papal portraits from Peter to Innocent I (401-417) are also attributed to him.

From that time onwards, restoration and embellishments advanced in relation to each pope's constant devotion to the Apostle of the Gentiles and veneration for the Basilica erected in his honour. At the end of the 5th century, under Pope Symmachus (498-514), the apse, which was in bad condition, was restructured, the Confession decorated and some *habitacula* (lodging rooms) constructed to offer hospitality to the poor and pilgrims.

In all likelihood, work was carried out on the presbytery area at the time of Gregory the Great (590-610) who raised the floor of the transept and connected it to the nave by means of five steps.

A semi-circular crypt, probably later destroyed under the pontificate of Leo III (795-816), was also opened behind the high altar and the tomb containing the remains of the Apostle. Sergius I (687-701) later repaired the roof of the Basilica and renovated the *cubicula* (bedrooms) of the *habitacula* of Pope Symmachus mentioned above.

Work resumed at the end of the 8th century, at the time of Hadrian I (772-795), when the lateral naves were restored and a new floor laid in the atrium.

This Pope also embellished the Basilica with liturgical ornamentation. His successor, Leo III (795-816), continued his work and also had the roof repaired, a marble floor laid and saw to the restoration of the apse vault, which, as the *Liber Pontificalis* mentions, was decorated with a mosaic like the one in the Vatican.

To protect the Basilica from pirate-like raids similar to the devastating Saracen attack in 846, John VIII (872-882) surrounded it with sturdy walls, following what Leo IV (847-855) had done to the Vatican in 848-849. The exact development or extension of the small citadel, called Giovannipoli in honour of the Pope, is unknown. However, it must have been fortified well enough to later withstand the repeated attacks of the Emperor Henry IV in 1083-1084.

Two important works were

Giovanni Paolo Panini, View of the Nave of the Basilica of Saint Paul, circa 1750 (Moscow, Pushkin Museum). Visible along the walls, above the famous series of papal portraits, are frescoes of scenes from the Acts of the Apostles and the Old Testament. The majority of them survived the fire, only to be destroyed during the rebuilding of the Basilica. The frescoes, attributed by Ghiberti to Pietro Cavallini, whose intervention during the last quarter of the thirteenth century left unaltered the iconographic programme of the old Leonine series, are primarily known because of copies which Cardinal Francesco Barberini had done in 1635. The paintings were executed along the wall in two parallel planes, each having twenty-two compartments. On the right are scenes from the Old Testament; on the left, stories from the Acts of the Apostles. Representations of the prophets appear between the windows above.

The Basilica of St. Paul Outside the Walls, an engraving by Jean Barbault, circa 1760. Visible are the 14th century bell tower and the 18th century portico which survived the 1823 fire, only to be destroyed in the rebuilding of the Basilica.

added to the Basilica during the 11th century: the bell tower, built next to the north nave, near the façade, and the bronze door of the main entrance, forged in Constantinople and donated by Pantaleone di Amalfi in 1070. In the meantime, Hildebrand of Soana, later to become Pope Gregory VII (1073-1085), reformed the monastery and restored the Church, while Abbot at Saint Paul's.

As a result of the fire which devastated the presbytery area in 1115, Pope Innocent II (1130-1143) had a wall built on columns for the whole length of the transept so as to support the unsafe roof, thus dividing it into two small naves. The Basilica had its greatest moment of splendour during the 13th century and the first quarter of the 14th century, at which time, Nicola D'Angelo and Pietro Vassalletto made the Paschal Candlestick; the

mosaic decoration of the bowl-shaped vault of the apse was carried out under Honorius III (1216-1227); the wonderful cloister was built (1208-1235); Pietro Cavallini did the cycle of paintings in the nave (which were to disappear during the 19th century rebuilding); Arnolfo di Cambio, *cum suo socio Petro* ("with his partner Peter") produced the priceless Altar Canopy; and, finally, the façade was decorated with a mosaic (1325). The Basilica was badly damaged during the 1349 earthquake, which also destroyed the bell tower and part of the portico. Pope Clemente VI (1342-1352), however, quickly undertook the restoration project.

At the beginning of the 14th century, when Boniface IX (1389-1404)—whose statue stands in the cloister—realized that the Church was falling into ruin, he set aside the total amount of indulgence offerings for its repair, a practice continued under Martin V (1417-1431). However, the work of restoring the *Ostiense* complex was begun only in 1426 in response to a proposal by Cardinal Gabriele Condulmer, the future Eugene IV (1431-1447).

The 16*th* century saw interventions by Gregory XIII (7572-1585) and Sixtus V (1585-1590). The former had the presbytery area decorated with paintings and the Apostle's tomb surrounded by a balustrade for the 1575 Jubilee Year; the latter had the presbytery area restored and added a coffered ceiling to the transept.

New altars were erected under Clement VIII (1592-1605), among them that of Saint Bridget and the high altar, attributed to Onorio Longhi. The Chapel of the Blessed Sacrament (today named in honour of Saint Lawrence) was erected by Carlo Maderno in 1619-1620 and decorated by Giovanni Lanfranco with frescoes and paintings having a Eucharistic theme..

Francesco Borromini's plan for the total restructuring of the Basilica can be dated at 1653, in response to the request of Innocent X (1644-1655), who shortly before had commissioned the Lombard architect to restore Saint John Lateran. His plan provided for the building of two semi-circular porticoes, at both the front and the back. The Pamphilj Pope, however, could only manage to start work on the new roof, later to be completed under Clement X (1670-1676). On 1 May 1724, to the embarrassment of the architect, Alessandro Specchi, the portico which he had recently erected suddenly collapsed. Pope Benedict XIII (1724-1730) immediately gave orders to Antonio Canevari to rebuild it for the approaching Holy Year celebration. In the course of work, the ancient narthex was destroyed and the surviving columns of the Paleo-Christian quadrangular portico were removed.

The Chapel of the Crucifix (today named in honour of the Blessed Sacrament), housing the venerated 14th century crucifix attributed at the time to Pietro Cavallini, was rebuilt in the same year. Finally, in 1747, Benedict XIV (1740-1758) restored the apse mosaic from which some fragments were taken (on view in the room near the Sacristy). He also oversaw the restoration of the cycle of frescoes by Cavallini and the series of papal portraits which was continued and completed by the painter, Salvatore Monosilio, to include the reigning Pope.

2. The 1823 Fire and Reconstruction

On the night between 15 and 16 July 1823, the ancient Basilica was ravaged by a terrible fire caused by the carelessness of workers who were restoring the roof. In a brief time flames destroyed most of the building. When the firemen arrived, they were confronted by "a spectacular sight [...] it was like a terrible Vesuvius, the lofty flames leapt higher than the highest mountains in their fatal dominion, this terrible accident could be seen for fifteen miles or more and every heart was filled with a sacred and penetrating horror" (C. Pietrangeli, *S. Paolo fuori le mura a Roma*, 1988, p. 67).

The net result was extremely serious. The central nave suffered the greatest damage. The roof caved in–the same fate occurred in the lateral naves and transept–, most of the left wall crumbled and some of the forty columns collapsed. The columns which had not fallen were irreparably damaged. The apse area, the triumphal arch (despite the threat of its falling), the dividing colonnades and the external walls of the lateral naves, the façade with its portico and the bell tower remained standing. While the transept walls seemed intact, the great dividing wall, erected by Innocent II (1130-1143) to support the roof, threatened to collapse.

Many of the works of art in the Basilica were also destroyed by the flames. Cavallini's frescoes, the series of papal portraits, the mosaics of the triumphal arch and the bowl-shaped vault in the apse and Arnolfo's Altar Canopy were all in urgent need of restoration.

A horrified and astonished Stendhal was among those who rushed to view the ruins which were extensively visually documented. In his work entitled *Roman Walks*, he describes it in the following manner: "I visited Saint Paul's the day after the fire. I had an impression of severe beauty, as sad as Mozart's music. The terrible, painful traces of the misfortune were still alive; the Church was still cluttered with half-burned, black smouldering beams; the trunks of the columns which were split from top to bottom threatened to fall down at any moment. The dismayed Romans had come out en masse to see the burned Church. It was one of the most overwhelming sights I had ever seen".

To comply with the wishes of the Pope's most trusted collaborators, the Secretary of State, Cardinal Consalvi being the first, Pope Pius VII (1800-1823), who was at the time advanced in years and ailing (he died

a little more than a month later on 20 August), never came to know of what happened. The arduous task of starting the rebuilding of the Basilica therefore passed to his successor, Leo XII (1823-1829), elected on 28 October, who immediately dedicated himself to the task. The architects were faced with difficult decisions, given both the exceptional importance of the building and the agonizing dilemma posed by the extensiveness of the damage. Should they rebuild the Basilica *in pristinum*, that is, maintaining the exact plan of the former one and reproducing the same architectural style, or should they create an entirely new building according to modern architectural theory?

A heated debate soon ensued with many people offering various designs and written opinions.

Architects like Giuseppe Valadier and Pasquale Belli, scholars like Carlo Fea and Angelo Uggeri and ordinary citizens equally took part.

Of particular interest is Valadier's plan, of which three versions are known from drawings and engravings. He proposed a 90-degree rotation of the façade, placing it in the west end of the transept; the old transept was to become the nave of the new Basilica and a second apse was to be opened opposite the old one, while the lateral naves and the portico of the original façade were to be used to house ancient monuments and provide space for processions within the building.

In the meantime, Pasquale Belli and Andrea Alippi set themselves to the urgent work of propping up the unsafe walls and closing off the two chapels dedicated to the Crucifix and the Blessed Sacrament, where religious services were continuing.

In September 1824, after much discussion, Giuseppe Valadier, willing to work for nothing as long as he could see his plan realized, was finally placed in charge of the rebuilding, with Salvi, Paccagnini and Alippi as his assistants.

Leo XII issued his Encyclical Letter *Ad Plurimas Easque*

Luigi Rossini, Interior of the Damaged Basilica, Viewed from the Entrance, 1823. The engraving, made shortly after the disastrous fire, appears with three others in the collection entitled "Roman Antiquities" in which the famed ruins are given the same importance as those of ancient Rome.

Gravissimas (25 January 1825) in order to face the immense expense estimated for what was to become the greatest construction site in Papal Rome in the 19th century. In the document, the Pope invited the bishops to promote a collection of offerings from the faithful to finance the rebuilding effort, much like Julius II had done for Saint Peter's. This urgent appeal, reiterated by Gregory XVI (1831-1846) in 1840, resulted in the sending of money (more than 400,000 *scudi* were collected) and precious materials, of which the gifts of the Viceroy of Egypt (alabaster columns) and Czar Nicolas I (blocks of malachite) are well-known.

On 23 November 1825 the special Reconstruction Commission, in response to the wishes of the Pope who had favoured the *in pristinum* rebuilding plan a few months earlier, removed Valadier from his position and placed Belli in charge, with Pietro Bosio, Andrea Alippi and Pietro Camporese the Younger as his assistants. The great opportunity for a new architectural design was thus lost and the rebuilding was resumed according to outmoded academic canons.

Where Belli conserved the old portico and façade, he destroyed most of the medieval remains.

However, the rather innovative idea of raising the nave floor was carried out by Luigi Poletti, who subsequently raised them approximately 90 centimetres.

The work of rebuilding began with the demolition of Galla Placidia's arch, once the valuable mosaic had been removed (September 1826), and its later reconstruction on massive columns of Montórfano granite, erected in the Summer of 1829. After the dividing wall of the transept was torn down (1826), the mosaic of the bowl-like vault in the apse was restored (1828). At the same time, the west walls of the transept and those of the central nave were demolished, thus destroying the Cavallini frescoes.

Gregory XVI ascended the papal throne in 1831, when the first of the eighty columns of the naves was being erected. He immediately showed a keen interest in the *Ostiense* building as testified by his numerous visits to the building site. Two years later, Luigi Poletti from Modena (1792-1869) succeeded Belli in directing the project, assisted by Bosio, Camporese and Virginio Vespignani (1808-1882).

Finally, on 5 October 1840, after a series of mishaps, the Pope was able to solemnly consecrate the Altar of Confession over which rose the restored Altar Canopy of Arnolfo. The transept, isolated from the naves, was to serve as the Basilica for the time being. By that date, the Blessed Sacrament and the Crucifix Chapels had already been restored and the Saints Stephen and Benedict Chapels, whose decoration was nearing completion, had been built next to them. The portico on the west end of the transept, which had served as a façade to the Basilica for a long time, was also finished. The construction of the bell tower, behind the apse, had begun (to be completed in 1860), and fifty-eight columns were standing in the naves.

In the course of the work, archeological discoveries were also made. In 1850, Vespignani undertook some surveying around the tomb of Saint Paul and Belloni discovered the apse of the early Constantine Basilica.

Work continued so rapidly in the pontificate of Pius IX (1846-1878) that the Pope was able to consecrate the new Basilica on 10 December 1854 in a lavish ceremony. Over the Altar of Confession, above Arnolfo's Altar Canopy, rose a still-more-imposing architectural canopy which was demolished in 1912 (the four columns are now part of the internal side of the Basilica's façade).

Though the plan for the new façade was approved in 1850, it took many years to reach completion. Filippo Agricola had drawn the designs for the mosaic in 1856, but the work on the narthex continued between 1873 and 1884 under Virginio Vespignani, the newly appointed person in charge of rebuilding, who also started the construction of the portico envisioned by Poletti.

The decoration of the walls of the naves and transept began in 1857 with the continuation and updating of the portraits of the popes and the painting of *Scenes from the Life of Saint Paul*, done by numerous artists of the Roman School.

After the unification of Italy, work slowed considerably and came to be completely suspended from 1884 to 14 March 1890, when the first stone of the quadrangular portico was laid. The portico was completed in 1928, as designed by Guglielmo Calderini, following an unfavourable judgment to Vespignani's plan.

The century-long, historical-artistic story of the reconstruction of the *Ostiense* Basilica concludes with the building of the quadrangular portico, the erection of Antonio Maraini's bronze door in 1931 and Arnaldo Foschini's construction, in those same years, of the Baptistry in a room adjacent to the south transept.

3. The Location

The Basilica lies between the *Via Ostiense*, which almost touches the eastward-facing apse, and the left bank of the Tiber, elements which, from antiquity, have greatly figured in the Basilica's relationship to the city of Rome in a dialectic and symbolic way. During the last two centuries, this situation changed with the construction of the Rome-Civitavecchia railway line (1862) and the raising of the banks of the Tiber (1930). The former interrupted the linear view of the Basilica walls and the latter, with the consequent disappearance of the Almone torrent, brought to an end the Basilica's often dramatic relationship with water.

Above:
The Basilica and its
quadrangular portico,
with the top of the bell
tower in the rear.

Right:
The Basilica as seen
from inside
the cloister.

*The massive statue of
Saint Paul by
Giuseppe Obici
(1807-1878),
located in the center
of the quadrangular
portico.*

4. The Quadrangular Portico

The majestic portico, in front of the façade, was built by Guglielmo Calderini between 1890 and 1928, developing Luigi Poletti's initial plan modified at his death in 1869 by Virginio Vespignani. From ancient times a porticoed atrium existed in front of the Basilica. The construction undertaken by Calderini, however, is entirely different and considerably larger. The northern and southern sections of the present portico, whose sides measure 70 metres in length, are closed off on the outside by travertine-covered walls. The western side, instead, opens onto the façade in a series of thirteen arches. Monumental propylaea join the sides of the portico at each corner. The imposing one hundred and fifty columns are arranged in a single line in the narthex, in two lines in the northern and southern sides and in three in the main front section, where paintings in the thirteen lunettes depict Christ giving his blessing, flanked by the Apostles. The portico's side walls are decorated with multi-coloured marbles and adorned with painted medallions depicting the symbols of the four Evangelists and Paleo-Christian symbols (vines, doves, an orb, deer, peacocks, etc).

*View of the façade
and the quadrangular
portico. On the upper
part of the façade
appear mosaics which
were done between
1854 and 1874 by
the Vatican Mosaic
Studio, based on
drawings by Filippo
Agricola and Nicola
Consoni. They depict
the prophets Isaiah,
Jeremiah, Ezekiel
and Daniel,
the Agnus Dei and
Christ with his hand
raised in blessing,
flanked by
the Apostles Peter
and Paul. Part of the
vestibule's rich,
painstakingly-done
decoration are the
doors of the three
main entrances (on
the right is the Holy
Door). The niches
contain statues of
Saints Peter and Paul
by Gregorio Zappalà
(1833-1908).*

5. The Gregorian Portico

The Gregorian Portico, so called because it was built by Luigi Poletti under Gregory XVI (1831-1846), is located at the northern end of the transept. Twelve columns recovered from the old Basilica were used in its construction, including the one bearing Pope Siricio's famous dedicatory inscription referring to the building of the Theodosian Basilica (19 November 390).

6. The Bell Tower

Erected by Luigi Poletti between 1840 and 1860, the Bell Tower rises in the rear, in line with the axis of the Basilica. With a height of about 65 metres, it is entirely covered with travertine marble and divided into 5 levels. On the southern and western sides of the second level—square in shape as the lower one—is the face of a clock made by Mariano Trevellini in 1863.

The next three levels, progressing in clear geometric forms laid one on top of the other, square-octagon-circle, follow the model of Alberti's towers, utilizing columns which correspond to the Doric-Ionic-Corinthian order. The final level takes the form of a small round monopteros temple with sixteen Corinthian columns and a high spherical vault on which is set a cross and orb. The inside of the bell tower, circular in form, has a diameter of 6 metres. A spiral travertine marble staircase, with two hundred and ninety-six steps, winds its way up from the ground level to the small temple. Seven bells are suspended inside the top three levels: two of the four bells, recovered from the old Basilica, were melted down in 1863 and 1930, the remaining two, dating back to 1658, were kept until 1959, when, according to the wishes of Pope John XXIII (1958-1963), the number of bells was increased.

7. The Bronze Door

The Bronze Door of the Basilica's main entrance was made by the sculptor Antonio Maraini (1886-1963) between 1929 and 1931, as indicated by the inscription at the bottom, where the dedication to the two Princes of the Apostles also appears.

Bl. Ildefonso Schuster (1880-1954), then Abbot of Saint Paul's, devised the door's iconographical plan based on the glory coming from the Apostles' preaching in the sign of the cross. Measuring an imposing 7.48 metres high and 3.35 metres wide,

the entire area is signed by a huge cross, composed of vine branches in silver damascening in which, suspended in ovals of lapislazuli, are engravings of the Apostles along the central edges of the double doors, and symbols of the Evangelists on the crosspiece. Church insignia (left) and that of the city of Rome (right) are represented in the uppermost panels. Each of the ten panels, five on each of the doors, depicts an event which took place in the city, with the exception of the two central panels dominated by the

Right and page 24:
Details from the
bronze door:
The Giving of the
Keys to Peter and The
Founding of
the Apostolic See; and
St. Paul's Arrival in
Rome as a Prisoner.

silver figure of Christ. These panels represent crucial moments in the lives of the two Apostles: *Christ Giving the Keys to Saint Peter and Saint Paul's Conversion on his Way to Damascus*.

On the right, progressing from bottom to top, are events from the life of Saint Paul: *Saint Paul Reaching Rome and his Welcome by the Roman Faithful; Saint Paul Making Conversions in Rome; The Conversion of the Centurion*; and *The Beheading of Saint Paul*; on the left, in the same order, are those related to the life of Saint Peter: *Saint Peter Baptizing in the Catacombs; The Founding of the Apostolic See; "Domine Quo Vadis?"*; and *The Crucifixion of Saint Peter*.

8. The Holy Door

Located to the right of the Basilica's main entrance, the new Holy Door, composed of two gilded bronze panels, was dedicated on 30 June 2000, replacing the former wooden one. Measuring 3.71 metres in height, 1.82 metres in width, and weighing 8 quintals, the door has a Trinitarian theme, conceived and executed by the sculptor Enrico Manfrini.

In the upper section, on the left, the mercy of God the Father is portrayed in the Parable of the Prodigal Son and the Good Samaritan; on the right, this attribute is reflected in the Pope who, in the foreground, extends his arms to embrace the poor and the sick. The colonnade of the Vatican Basilica in the background, with its outstretched arms, is a symbol of welcome.

In the middle section, on the left, God the Holy Spirit descends on the Virgin Mary and the Apostles at Pentecost, while, on the right, his work continues in the evangelization of peoples, particularly through Saint Paul, who undergoes martyrdom in the lower, left-hand corner.

In the lower section, on the left, the Redemption of humanity is accomplished by God the Son, through his death on the cross; on the right, his work of salvation is continued through the ages by the bishops who guide humanity to the font of life.

Finally, at the base, the two-line inscription is a greeting to all visitors of the Pauline Basilica, wishing them the gift of peace and eternal salvation: *Ad sacram Pauli cunctis venientibus aedem – sit pacis donum perpetuoque salus* ("May the gift of peace and eternal salvation be granted to all who come to Paul's holy temple").

*The Holy Door
by the sculptor
Enrico Manfrini.*

AD SACRAM PAVLI CVNCTIS VENIENTIBVS AEDEM

SIT PACIS DONVM PERPETVOQVE SALVS

Following the plan of a Tau cross, the Basilica is divided into five naves by four rows of twenty columns and a raised transept, and measures 131 metres long, 65 metres wide and 30 metres high.

Work on the interior, begun by Pasquale Belli, continued from 1831 to 1854 under Luigi Poletti, who was in charge of the work of restoration from 1833 until his death in1869. The central nave is bound by forty archivolted columns of Baveno granite with white Carrara marble Corinthian capitals. Above the frieze-like area of papal portraits, between Corinthian pilasters, murals depicting scenes from the life of Saint Paul alternate with arched windows. The inside of the Basilica's façade is decorated with six alabaster columns donated by the Egyptian Viceroy, Mohamed Alì, in1840. The two central columns bear the massive marble coat-of-arms of Pius IX (1846-1878), the work of Giosuè Meli, which is supported by two, winged figures sculptured by Ignazio Iacometti and Salvatore Revelli. Incorporating materials recovered from the ancient Basilica, the floor of the naves and of the transept resembles an immense carpet of precious marbles. The coats-of-arms of the Popes associated with the history of the building appear in the rich, gold coffered ceilings. Along the walls of the central nave, the two smaller naves and the transept are large arched windows, inset with thin panels of alabaster, donated by King Fuad I of Egypt. In the massive niches in the walls of the two outer naves are the statues of ten Apostles (five on each side) which, together with those of Saint Peter and Saint Paul on pedestals in the central nave, were sculptured in 1882 by artists such as A. Allegretti, F. Fabi-Altini, E. Gallori and E. Maccagnani, who followed exacting academic theory.

Following pages: View of the interior of the Basilica with the double colonnade of Corinthian columns.

The solemn and majestic central nave, viewed from the transept.

Details from the transept's and nave's wooden ceiling.
Above: The coat-of-arms of Gregory XVI (1831-1846).
Below: The coat-of-arms of Pius IX (1846-1878).

10. The Byzantine Door

In 1967, the splendid Byzantine Door, used in the main entrance of the Basilica before the fire, occupied the place of the Holy Door. The Latin and Greek inscriptions indicate that it was commissioned by the Consul Pantaleone di Amalfi (portrayed in one of the panels) in Constantinople and was produced in 1070 by an artist named Teodoro. For a long time, the work was attributed to Staurachio, who was only involved in its casting.

The double doors, which suffered serious damage in the 1823 fire, are divided into six vertical strips with 54 panels, some of which were partially restored in 1965-66 (four were lost).

The panels develop a complex iconographical plan with twelve Christological scenes (from the Nativity to Pentecost), the twelve Apostles and scenes of their martyrdom, twelve prophets, two eagles, two crosses and two panels with two dedicatory inscriptions in Latin, all of which is done in silver damascening.

The door is a rather fine example of the artistry existent at that time.

Details from the Byzantine Door: The Martyrdom of Saints Peter and The Martyrdom of St. Paul.

Key to the Iconographic Subjects on the Byzantine Door

Left Side

1. The Annunciation
2. The Birth of Jesus Christ
3. The Presentation
4. The Baptism of Jesus Christ
5. The Transfiguration
6. The Entry into Jerusalem
7. The Crucifixion
8. The Deposition from the Cross
9. The Resurrection
10. The Apparition to the Apostles
11. The Ascension
12. Pentecost
13. The Cross
14. The Inscription *Tu quoque*
15. The Martyrdom of Saint Paul
16. Jesus, Saint Paul, Saint Pantaleon
17. The Martyrdom of Saint Peter
18. St. Peter
19. The Martyrdom of Saint Andrew
20. Saint Andrew
21. The Burial of Saint John
22. Saint John the Theologian
23. The Martyrdom
    of Saint Bartholomew
24. The Eagle
25. Saint Thomas
27. The Martyrdom of Saint Thomas

Right Side

*Details from
the Byzantine Door:
The Crucifixion
of Christ and Saint Peter.*

11. *The Papal Portraits*

Above the naves and the transept is the series of Papal Portraits, reconstructed from the famous series in the ancient Basilica begun in the 5th century by Pope Leo the Great (440-461), continued by Cavallini at the end of the 13th century and followed by Benedict XIV (1740-1758) during the work of preparation for the Holy Year 1750. The forty-one, only-surviving portraits of this original series, documented in the Vatican Latin Code 4407, are now kept in the Basilica Museum. In May, 1847 Pius IX (1846-1878) directed that the work of replacing the old series was to be done in mosaic rather than fresco. Filippo Agricola, the Director of the Vatican Mosaic Studio, was assigned the task of determining the papal likenesses. Many painters were involved in the work, some of which were employed in the series of frescoes on scenes from the life of Saint Paul, for example, Bompiani, Canterani, De Rossi, Trojetti, Podesti and Sozzi. Work on the oil-painting models, presently kept in the Fabric of Saint Peter's, was completed in two years, while their realization in mosaic continued to 1876. The series is updated with each new Pope.

12. The Pauline Series

Above the Papal Portraits and set between Corinthian pilasters, thirty-six frescoes, depicting *Scenes from the Life of Saint Paul* from the Acts of the Apostles, alternate with windows along the walls of the central nave and transept. This series of frescoes was commissioned by Pius IX (1846-1878) in 1857 to replace those of Cavallini which had been destroyed. The work was completed in only three years by a group of twenty-two artists, including Francesco Podesti, Pietro Gagliardi, Carlo Gavardini, Francesco Coghetti and Francesco Grandi, all deserving mention because of the quality of their work. Each painting is framed in marble; above are paintings of putti holding a shield bearing the Latin title of the scene. Arranged in chronological order, the scenes begin in the transept to the right of the apse, in the first set of pilasters, continue in the nave and conclude in the left transept.

The scenes are as follows: *Saul, Persecutor of Christians, Present at the Martyrdom of Saint Stephen* and *The Conversion of Saul*, both paintings by Pietro Gagliardi (1809-1890); *Ananias Lays Hands on Saul Who Receives the Virtues of the Holy Spirit* and *Ananias Baptizes Saul* by Francesco Podesti (1800-1895); *Paul Preaches in Damascus and Paul Flees from Damascus* by Guglielmo De Sanctis (1829-1911); *Paul Among the Apostles at the Council of Jerusalem* by Nicola Consoni (1814-1884); *The Consecration of Paul and Barnabus, Paul Converts Sergius, Proconsul of Paphos, Paul and Barnabus in Lystra* and *The Stoning of Paul in Lystra* by Cesare Mariani (1826-1901); *Paul's Vision in Troas* and *Paul Exorcises a Young Girl in Philippi* by Luigi Cochetti (1802-1884); *Paul and Silas Are Flogged in Philippi* by Vincenzo Morani (1809-1870); *Paul Converts the Jailer in Philippi* by Giuseppe Sereni; *Paul's Speech in the Aeropagus of Athens* by Giovan Battista Pianello (1812-after 1866); *Paul in Corinth* by Domenico Tojetti (1831-1901 ca.); *The Converted Ephesians Burn their Scrolls* by Casimiro De Rossi; *Paul Brings the Young Eutychus Back to Life* by Natale Carta (1790-1884); *Paul Leaves for Miletus* by Marcello Sozzi; *The Prophecy of Agabus* by Roberto Bompiani (1821-1908); *Paul and James in Jerusalem*, by Cesare Dies (1830-after 1884); *Paul is Expelled from the Temple in Jerusalem and Paul's Speech to the People of Jerusalem* by Francesco Grandi (1831-1891); *Paul Declares Himself to be a Roman and Escapes Flogging in Jerusalem* by Natale Carta; *Paul's Vision in Jerusalem and Paul before Felix in Caesarea* by Domenico Bartolini; *Paul's Shipwreck in Cauda and Paul and The Viper in Malta* by Achille Scaccioni; *Paul Cures the Father of Publius, Prince of Malta* by Nicola Consoni; *Paul Meets the Christians of Rome on the Appian Way and Paul in*

Rome by Carlo Gavardini; *Paul's Elevation to the Third Heaven and Peter and Paul in the Mammertine Prison* by Francesco Coghetti (1802-1875); *Peter and Paul Embrace before their Martyrdom and The Martyrdom of Saint Paul* by Filippo Baldi.

Filippo Balbi, Peter and Paul Embrace Before Their Martyrdom.

13. The Mosaics

The mosaic of the triumphal arch, called the mosaic of Galla Placidia, after the sister of Emperor Honorius who financed the work, was made under the pontificate of Saint Leo the Great (440-461), at the same time as the one in the Basilica of Saint Mary Major.

The mosaic work was completely redone between the 8th and 9th centuries, as seen by comparing it with that in the Church of Saints Nereus and Achilles. Unfortunately, because of various insufficient attempts at restoration, the present mosaic does not reflect its ancient splendour. In the central *clipeus* Christ is giving a blessing, flanked by two angels and symbols of the Evangelists. The Twenty-Four Elders from the Book of Revelation are portrayed, twelve on each side, with the Apostles Peter and Paul appearing below each group. Seriously damaged by the 1823 fire, the triumphal arch was rebuilt on two massive columns of Montórfano granite (14 metres high), after removing the mosaic and later replacing it in 1853.

A portion of the mosaic decoration from the façade of the ancient Basilica was placed on the backside of the triumphal arch; the remaining parts were incorporated in the transept, on both sides of the apse mosaic. Commissioned by Pope John XXII (1316-1334) in 1325, the mosaic was again attributed by Ghiberti to Pietro Cavallini. A satisfactory analysis of style cannot be done with any certainty, however, because of the extensive 19th century restoration work and the fact that the mosaic was in a deteriorated state before the fire.

In ancient times the mosaic on the façade was divided as follows: the *clipeus* was in the tympanum, supported by two angels, with Christ giving a blessing and the symbols of the four Evangelists, two on each side. Mosaics of Saint Paul, a Madonna and Child, Saint John the Baptist and Saint Peter appeared in the lower part, between the windows.

The great mosaic in the bowl-like vault of the apse also suffered great damage during the fire in the Basilica; indeed almost the entire mosaic was replaced using little of the ancient tesserae. A few original fragments portraying the heads of the apostles and bird-designs can be seen in areas adjoining the Basilica. Documentation indicates that the apse mosaic was made in the second and third decade of the 13th century by Venetian workmen called to Rome by Pope Honorius III (1216-1227), a fact confirmed by the affinity in style with the mosaics of Saint Mark's Basilica in Venice. The mosaic work in Saint Paul's, together with that in the apse of the Vatican, marked the resumption of a great mosaic tradition in the city which would culminate at the end of the century with work in the major Roman Basilicas.

In the apse, Christ is in the centre, seated on his throne, and Pope

Following pages: Detail from the backside of the triumphal arch.

Apse Mosaic commissioned by Honorius III and executed between 1220 and 1230.

Honorius III prostrate at his feet, with Saint Peter and Saint Andrew to his left, and, to his right, Saint Paul and Saint Luke. The figures stand in field resplendent with flowers and various animals. Beneath is a representation of the *Hetimasia* (the empty throne with the cross and the instruments of Christ's passion), flanked by angels. Between the angels, at their feet, are seven almost undetectable figures, five representing the Holy Innocents and two kneeling characters from that time: Adinolfo, the Sacristan, and Giovanni Caetani, the Abbot. Apostles and Saints appear at the sides: on the right,

Jacob, Bartholemew, Thomas, Simon, Matthias and Mark; and, on the left, John, Phillip, Matthew, Jacob the Younger, Thaddaeus and Barnabas.

The central portion of the mosaic, from the base of the throne to the representation of the *Hetimasia* and the figure of Pope Honorius III, can be said with certainty to be original.

Memorial tablets with the names of various people who took part in the consecration of the Basilica are positioned along the apse walls. Coming from every part of the world, the participants assembled in Rome on 10 December 1854 for the proclamation

Below:
*The triumphal arch
and the apse area.*

Opposite:
*The apse vault with
the papal cathedra.*

of the dogma of the Immaculate Conception: the entire College of Cardinals, the Patriarch of Alexandria and a grand total of 140 bishops. In the centre stands the rich marble throne designed by Poletti, on the back of which is a relief by Pietro Tenerani, depicting *Christ Giving the Keys to Saint Peter.*

Fragments of the apse mosaic removed after the 1823 fire and presently kept in the Gregorian Room next to the sacristy of the Basilica: apostle's head, perhaps Saint Simon (above); apostle's head (belowe).

14. The Tomb of Saint Paul

The Confession, the burial place of Saint Paul the Apostle, the most sacred spot in the Basilica, lies below the papal altar over which rises Arnolfo's Altar Canopy. The *hypogeum*, reached by a double staircase, is surrounded by a white marble balustrade with reproductions of the Paleo-Christian partitions. The bronze doors of the small entrance bear the likenesses of Timothy and Titus, disciples of Saint Paul, by Pietro Tenerani. The porphyry table of the papal altar holds the remains of Saint Timothy the Martyr.

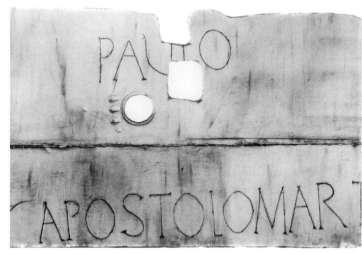

Above: The marble slab from the tomb of Saint Paul (4th - 5th century) below the high altar.

A plaster reproduction is in the Basilica's Picture Gallery.

Below: The grating looking on the tomb of Saint Paul.

15. The Altar Canopy

The splendid Gothic Altar Canopy by Arnolfo di Cambio rises above the papal altar, so called, because only the Pope can celebrate there (on very rare occasions also the Abbot of Saint Paul's). As a result of the damage it suffered in the 1823 fire, that is, the calcination of the four porphyry support columns (later replaced) and the semi-destruction of some of the decorative elements of the small roof, the Altar Canopy was dismantled, restored and then remounted in its original position. During the process, it was discovered that Arnolfo had used ancient blocks of marble for his work, some of which bore inscriptions.

Trefoil ogival arches, surmounted by triangular tympana with pinnacles at the sides and decorated with angels bearing a small rosette in a mosaic background, are mounted on the richly ornate capitals of four porphyry columns. The bas-reliefs in the spraddles portray Adam and Eve, the Offering of Cain and Abel, Abbot Bartholomew offering the Altar Canopy to Saint Paul and a scene with two unidentified characters.

In the corner niches, between the small columns, are statues of Saints Peter, Paul, Timothy and Benedict. The Canopy's roof has, in the centre, a small shrine with a spire and pinnacles at each corner. Rich mosaics adorn the internal sections, including animals within roundels, some of which are flanked by canthari, while four, sometimes-boldly-foreshortened angels with candlesticks and thuribles are placed in the springer-corners of the vault. The inscriptions on the front, facing the nave, note that the Altar Canopy was built in 1285 by Arnolfo di Cambio, who was commissioned by Bartholomew, Abbot of the monastery from 1282-1297. A certain Pietro, known as "his partner," served as his assistant. In the past, he was thought to be Pietro Cavallini, but recent scholarship has identified him as Pietro di Oderisio. The hand of each man is distinguishable in the work as well as that of the assistants of the workshop. Besides the general style, the small corner statues and other minor elements can be attributed to Arnolfo with certainty. The Altar Canopy of Saint Paul's, because of its innovative sculptural language and architectural elements which bear novel Gothic features—a forerunner to the one in Saint Cecilia's in Trastevere also by Arnolfo—was the beginning of a new artistic tradition, making Rome one of the foremost centres of art in Italy at the end of the 13th century with works done by Jacopo Torriti, Pietro Cavallini, Giotto and Arnolfo di Cambio.

Left: The Altar Canopy with the artists' names and the dedication to its commissioner. Right: An angel with candlestick in the interior of the vault.

16. The Paschal Candlestick

This type of candlestick, designed to hold the Easter Candle and to be placed near the altar in *cornu evangeli*, has become a fundamental element of the Holy Saturday Liturgy since the 10th century. The one in Saint Paul's is particularly unique, being a splendid example of the craftsmanship of marble cutters who created their own sculptural school in Rome between the 11th and 13th centuries. Indeed, its imposing character comes from its colossal size (5.60 metres in height) and from the fact that its surface is completely carved. The tall shaft, subdivided horizontally into six sections, stands on a base of alternating female and animal figures, some of the latter bearing human faces. The first section is decorated with plant and animal motifs; the last two sections bear plant arabesques; and those in-between portray the following scenes taken from Christ's Passion and Resurrection: *Christ before Caiphas, The Mocking of Christ, Christ before Pilate, Pilate Washing his Hands, The Crucifixion, The Resurrection* and *The Ascension.* At the top, the huge cup meant to support the candle is carried by a ring of monstrous animals. The sculpture is clearly consistent with the tradition of Paleo-Christian art as well as the developing Romanesque culture of the time; it also stands in succession to the decorative forms of the spiral columns of antiquity. The names of the two artists responsible for the work are written below the series of scenes from Christ's life: Nicola D'Angelo, who in all likelihood was responsible for the general design of the work, and Pietro Vassalletto, both members of important families of marble-carvers. This information is of particular importance in dating the work between the end of the 12ᵗʰ century and the beginning of the 13ᵗʰ and thereby creating a reference point in the history of Roman sculpture.

Detail:
The Crucifixion.

17. The Transept

At the ends of the transept are two identical altars, composed of four Corinthian columns of *paonazzetto* marble, supporting an architrave with an inscription. On the right is the altar of Our Lady of the Assumption where a statue of Saint Benedict by Filippo Gnaccarini and that of Saint Scholastica by Felice Baini flank the mosaic done by the Vatican Mosaic Studio—a reproduction of the *Assumption of Our Lady*, believed to be from Monteluce, done by Giulio Romano and Penni, based on a drawing by Raphael and now kept in the Vatican Picture Gallery. On the left is the altar of the Conversion of Saint Paul with a statue of Saint Gregory the Great by Francesco Massimiliano Laboureur, pupil of Thorvaldsen, and that of Saint Bernard, done by Achille Stocchi in 1836. Vincenzo Camuccini's painting of *The Conversion of Saint Paul* is above the altar. The two altars, composed of malachite (donated by Czar Nicholas I) and lapis lazuli and supported at their corners by gold-plated, bronze angels, are of considerable value. The four chapels off the transept, each with a different plan and construction date, are united in sharing the same rich, multi-coloured doors built in 1928 by the architect, Foschini.

The altar of the Assumption.

18. The Saint Stephen Chapel

Built by Poletti during the work done on the transept, the Saint Stephen Chapel is dedicated to the protomartyr who, in the Acts of the Apostles, is responsible for St. Paul's conversion. The marble work, in part utilizing materials from the ancient Basilica, was nearing completion in 1847. The walls of the rectangular Chapel are divided by pilasters of red granite, resting on a high, base-board moulding of African breccia marble. These pilasters are topped by Corinthian capitals with precious marble panels in between. The statue of Saint Stephen on the altar is the work of Rinaldo Rinaldi (1793-1873), a mediocre disciple of Canova. Two altar-pieces, commissioned by Gregory XVI in 1845, are in the centre of the side walls. The one on the left depicts *Saint Stephen Condemned by the Sanhedrin* by Francesco Coghetti and the one on the right portrays *The Stoning of Saint Stephen* by Francesco Podesti.

The altar wall.

19. The Blessed Sacrament Chapel

*The altar wall;
Rigth, The revered
wooden statue of
Saint Paul.*

The Blessed Sacrament Chapel was rebuilt for the 1725 Jubilee Year to house the venerated 14th century, wooden Crucifix thought then to be the work of Pietro Cavallini. Surviving the fated fire, the Chapel maintains its original baroque form: a rectangular plan with concave angles, straight apse and eight wall niches. The wooden Crucifix, attributed by Vasari to Cavallini, hangs above the altar. However, because of the meticulous restoration work done to the Crucifix from 1972-1974, during which the original polychrome work was retraced, it is now agreed that the work belongs to the Sienese school active at the beginning of the 14th century. Statues occupy the niches: four golden stucco angels are in the side niches; and in the corner ones, next to the entrance, on the left, is the venerated wooden statue of Saint Paul, which is continually scratched by the pilgrims who want to take away splinters as relics, and, on the right, is the

statue of Saint Bridget attributed to Stefano Maderno (1576-1636). Saint Bridget is represented kneeling with arms outstretched towards the Crucifix, where, according to tradition, Christ turned his head to her as she was deep in prayer at his feet. The Chapel also holds a venerated 13th century mosaic depicting a *Madonna and Child*.

Left: The mosaic icon of the Theotokos Hodigitria ("Mother of God, Showing the Way") in typical Byzantine style (13ᵗʰ century).
In 1541, before this image, Saint Ignatius of Loyola, together with some of his followers, made their profession, thus beginning the work of the Company of Jesus.
Right:
The wooden crucifix (14ᵗʰ century).

20. The Saint Lawrence Chapel

Constructed by Carlo Maderno in 1619-1620 and formerly dedicated to the Blessed Sacrament, the Saint Lawrence Chapel has walls decorated with eight paintings by Lanfranco, the artist of the frescoes in the lunettes and the altar pieces as well. The paintings depict scenes from the Old and New Testament; the vault bears Sibyls and Prophets by the Florentine artist, Anastasio Fontebuoni. The restoration work following the fire was completed in 1852. The vault was decorated by Antonio Viligiardi (1869-1936) at the beginning of the century with scenes from the life of Saint Lawrence, surrounded by angels in flight. The walls are lined with choir-stalls, designed by Calderini and executed by the Perugian engraver, A. Monteneri. On the back panels, set in fanciful architectural designs are the likenesses of Saints and the two Princes of the Apostles. The marble relief on the front of the altar comes from the inside of the Basilica's façade and can be dated between the end of the 15th century and the beginning of the 16th century. Saint Anthony Abbot, Saint Dionysius and Saint Justina appear in its three shell-shaped niches.

Right: The altar wall with the 14th century relief, attributed to the School of Andrea Bregno.

21. The Saint Benedict Chapel

The Saint Benedict Chapel, built in the right transept by Luigi Poletti in 1843-1845, has a rectangular plan (17.67 metres x 8.50 metres) and a rectangular apse. Its interior is decorated with twelve ash-grey marble columns found during the excavations done in 1811-1812 in the ancient Veio district at *Isola Farnese*. In 1824, Leo XII (1823-1829) had what was found brought to Rome and Gregory XVI (1835) donated the materials to the Basilica. Each of the 2.90 metre, 20-faceted columns has composite capitals (11 originals and 1 copy) which are decorated with stylized leaves and flowers. The statue of Saint Benedict by Pietro Tenerani (1789-1869) stands on a high pedestal in the niche.

Right: The statue of Saint Benedict by Pietro Tenerani (1789-1869). Opposite: The marble holy water font of Pietro Galli, sculptured for the Duchess of Beuffremount who donated it to Pius IX in 1860.

22. The Baptistry

Built by Arnaldo Foschini in 1930, the Baptistry stands in an ancient room between the Saint Julian Oratory and the Sacristy. His plan replaced the small octagonal temple with a double row of columns–never built–which Poletti had designed for the square in front of the Basilica. Devised in an equilateral cross plan, the centre, positioned below the level of the old Basilica, can be reached by means of steps. The arches, supported by columns with ionic and pulvin capitals along the walls, are original. The undersides of the arches bear frescoes with the likenesses of Saints and the coats-of-arms of the Basilica can be seen amidst 15th century geometric and floral motifs. The walls and floor are in polychro-matic marble, while the baptismal font in the centre of the room is decorated with symbolic animals in malachite, lapis lazuli and mother-of-pearl. A frescoed frieze runs underneath the four arches. Amidst a rich leafy decoration, twelve rectangular and circular compartments display busts of the Evangelists, the Doctors of the Church, God the Father, Saint Peter and Saint Paul and an unidentified Martyr-Saint. The frescoes, agreed to be from the hand of Antonio da Viterbo, can be dated from 1460 to 1465. In 1451-1452, the Benedictine Order had previously commissioned him to paint the Triptych of the Redeemer in the Church of *Santa Maria delle Grazie* in Capena, which was under the authority of the *Ostiense* monastery.

Opposite: The baptismal font.

*Frescoes depicting the Apostles Peter and Paul,
attributed to Antonio da Viterbo.*

23. The Saint Julian Oratory

The Saint Julian Oratory, also known as the Martyr Room, acts as a passageway between the transept of the Basilica and the Cloister. The frescoes along the walls, even though they have been repainted more than once, can be dated between the end of the 12th century and the beginning of the 14th century.

The Saint Julian Oratory, The Crucifixion.

The Saint Julian Oratory, The Holy Martyrs.

24. The Cloister

The cloister, a jewel of Cosmati art and the most significant surviving part of the ancient monastery complex, adjoins the south transept of the Basilica. The four ambulatories meander around the rectangular garden, accessible from each side. They are bound by a low podium on which rises a series of small double columns, four to each span, supporting small rounded arches which bear the splendid pediment decorated with mosaics—a unique part of the cloister—and the elaborate cornice with the heads of animals.

The northern side, adjoining the Basilica, stands in contrast to the great simplicity of the other three sides, because of its rich, varied decoration. Its columns have a large variety of shapes and forms—smooth, fluted, spiral and twisted—and are very often inlaid with mosaics. The space between the small arches is attentively decorated on both the outer and inner surfaces with a succession of symbols, *flora* and *fauna* designs and monstrous, fanciful beings (leaf masks, chimeras, a face with three foreheads, "a wolf at school", etc.), which have a clear, moral intent, though lacking a general iconographical plan. The floral motif continues along the entire cornice, interrupted at intervals by sculptures of animals and, in some cases, human heads, while the coffered undersides of the arches are decorated with stylized rosettes. All these elements indicate that the author of the northern side possessed a more varied cultural background and figurative language beyond the obvious classical references from eastern and Etruscan sources, thus revealing that the cloister is the work of two different artists and two distinct periods of construction. The inscription on the eastern, southern and western sides of the architrave, illustrating the beauty and the conducive nature of the place for study and prayer, states that the cloister was begun by the Amalfi Cardinal, Pietro di Capua, and completed by Giovanni Caetani di Ardea, the Abbot of Saint Paul's from 1212 to 1235. Comparing the stylistic elements of the cloister to those of the cloister of Saint John Lateran from the same period, permits dating the cloister to approximately 1208-1210 and 1230-1235. Indications lead to the belief that the northern side was built later than the other three sides and after the cloister of the Lateran (completed in 1227). It does share enough obvious similarities with that of the Lateran to identify it with the workshop of Vassalletto, in particular "Vassalletto's son", Pietro—also the author of the *Ostiense* Paschal Candlestick—who brought to completion the work on

Following pages: The western side of the cloister.

*Below: The first
two spans
of the northern side
of the cloister.
Opposite:
The ambulatory of
the northern side of
the cloister.*

the Lateran cloister begun by his father. Many doubts still remain concerning the other sides of the cloister. However, from all indications, theories attributing the work to Pietro de Maria, author of the cloister of Sassovivo near Foligno, or more recently to the joint workmanship of Pietro Vassalletto and Nicola d'Angelo, after their completion of the Paschal Candlestick, seem totally unfounded.

Right: Adam and Eve tempted by the serpent.

Opposite: A chimera

Above: Sarcophagus, 3ʳᵈ century, used in the 12ᵗʰ century as the tomb of Pierleoni. On the front is the procession of the Muses; on the left side, Apollo playing the lyre; on the right side, the torture of Marsia.

Opposite: Statue of Pope Boniface IX, family-name Tomacelli (1389-1404), who lavished works on the Basilica; according to some, the statue was executed for the Jubilee Year 1400.

BONIFATIO·IX·TOMACELLO
PONT·OPT·MAX
GRATI·ANIMI·MONVMENTVM
A·CASINENSI·CONGREGATIONE
OLIM·ERECTVM
MOX·TEMPORVM·INIVRIA
COLLAPSVM
LVCRETIA·TOMACELLA
COLVMNA
PALIANI·DVX
GENTILI·SVO·RESTITVIT

25. The Picture Gallery

The Basilica Picture Gallery is located in the room adjoining the sacristy and in two small rooms nearby. It holds about forty paintings, of considerable historical-artistic value, dating from the 13th to the 19th century.

Antoniazzo Romano, Madonna with Child and Saints Benedict, Paul, Peter and Justina, tempera on wood, datable from 1480 to 1485. The presence of Saint Justina leads to the belief that the painting was commissioned to commemorate the union, in 1426, between the monastery of Saint Paul and the Congregation of Padua bearing her name.

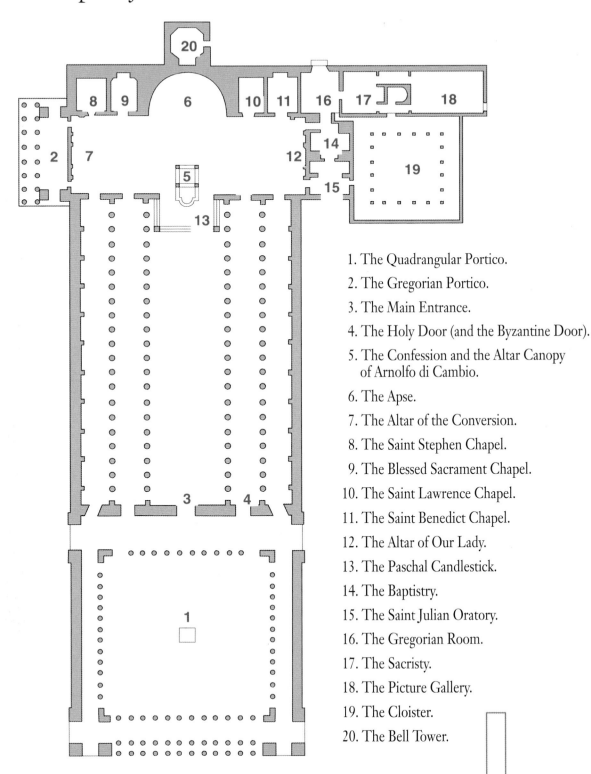

1. The Quadrangular Portico.
2. The Gregorian Portico.
3. The Main Entrance.
4. The Holy Door (and the Byzantine Door).
5. The Confession and the Altar Canopy of Arnolfo di Cambio.
6. The Apse.
7. The Altar of the Conversion.
8. The Saint Stephen Chapel.
9. The Blessed Sacrament Chapel.
10. The Saint Lawrence Chapel.
11. The Saint Benedict Chapel.
12. The Altar of Our Lady.
13. The Paschal Candlestick.
14. The Baptistry.
15. The Saint Julian Oratory.
16. The Gregorian Room.
17. The Sacristy.
18. The Picture Gallery.
19. The Cloister.
20. The Bell Tower.

Index